A History
of the
Canadian
Constitution

from 1864 to the Present

Jean-François Cardin

A History
of the
Canadian
Constitution

from 1864 to the Present

Translated by
Diana Halfpenny

GLOBAL VISION

Series Editor   René Jones
Translation   Diana Halfpenny
Editor   Mark Bourrie
Layout   Isabelle Jones
Proofreading   Frank Manley

Canadian Cataloguing in Publication Data

Cardin, Jean-François
A history of the Canadian Constitution: from 1864 to the present
(Spotlight)
Translation of: Histoire de la Constitution canadienne.
ISBN 2-9804592-2-4
1. Canada - Constitutional history.
2. Canada - Constitution - Amendments.
3. Canada - Politics and government - 1867-.
4. Federal-provincial relations - Canada.
5. Nationalism - Canada.
I. Title. II. Series: Spotlight (Montréal, Québec)
JL61.C3713 1996   342.71'029   C96-941065-4

Global Vision Publishing Company
5152 King-Edward Avenue
Montreal, Quebec
Canada H4V 2J7
Tel.: (514) 488-7435

Legal deposit: 4th quarter 1996
Bibliothèque nationale du Québec
National Library of Canada
ISBN 2-9804592-2-4

(French version: ISBN 2-9804592-1-6, © 1995 Les Éditions Vision Globale)

TABLE OF CONTENTS

INTRODUCTION TO THE SERIES

Although we are constantly bombarded with information from radio, newspapers and television, we are not always able to fully grasp what is happening at home and abroad.

Why?

Because the news these media provide is often incomplete: instead of offering thought-provoking, in-depth coverage, their main objective is to make the headlines, or deliver the top story on the late-night television news.

People often feel powerless when there are crises or conflicts in the news. They are quite literally overwhelmed by the events they see, hear or read about, not because of a lack of information, but because there is too much of the wrong kind. In order to truly understand what is happening, they need to know more.

Even so, there is no lack of reference material. Libraries are crammed with scholarly works, dealing with every subject under the sun. However, many of us simply cannot find time for this kind of reading. It was this very observation that gave rise to "Spotlight," a series of short books, written for the general public, that explore the historical background of current events.

In a simple and straightforward manner, we hope to explain the present by recalling the past. Our aim is to provide our readers with reading and reference material that will enable them to form an enlightened opinion of the daily events in the news.

The constitutional history of Canada (Canadian political issues at the dawn of the 21st century) is the first in the series. The crisis in Yugoslavia (different kinds of nationalism), and in Algeria (Muslim fundamentalism) will follow.

Our only ambition is to make our readers want to know more, learn more and better understand the world in which they live.

INTRODUCTION

The constitutional debate between the federal government and the provinces started not long after Confederation. The Dominion of Canada was proclaimed on July 1, 1867, and shortly thereafter, the struggle for power began.

At the heart of the problem was the Canadian Constitution itself: a double-edged sword that has sustained the constitutional debate for over 125 years. At first, this debate was purely political but it has come to permeate every level of society, creating tension among the "founding peoples": English Canada on the one side, Quebec on the other and, between the two, the native peoples, who have more recently been making their voices heard.

How exactly did this constitutional impasse come about? To answer this question, we must take a closer look at the origin and evolution of the Canadian Constitution itself.

CHAPTER I

The Birth of Confederation 1864 – 1867

The 1850s and 1860s were years of sweeping economic change for the British colonies of North America. The Province of Canada, made up of Canada East (Quebec) and Canada West (Ontario), as well as New Brunswick, Nova Scotia, Prince Edward Island and Newfoundland were considering political union as a means of giving birth to a new country.

The Beginnings of Confederation

THE POLITICAL SITUATION in the Province of Canada had been in turmoil since the end of the 1850s. The 1840 Act of Union, uniting Upper and Lower Canada (Ontario and Quebec, respectively), had created two major sources of conflict: the first was between two political factions, the Reformers and the Conservatives. The second and more serious division was between English and French Canadians. Three general elections were held between 1858 and 1864. Six governments came and went in rapid succession; the Province of Canada was in a political deadlock. The Reformers, headed by George Brown, held the majority of seats in Canada West (Ontario).

However, George Brown's plans for reform were blocked by an alliance between the Conservatives in Canada West, led by John A. Macdonald, and those in Canada East (Quebec) led by George-Étienne Cartier.

THE ECONOMIC SITUATION was such that the urban centres of the Province of Canada were becoming more and more industrialized. Due to the increasing difficulty of reaching British and American markets, the ideal solution for many appeared to be the creation of an internal market that would include all the British colonies of North America. Railroad construction—begun in the 1840s and continuing throughout the next decade—had left the government of the Province of Canada heavily in debt, preventing it from undertaking any of the large projects it had envisioned. Building a whole network of railroads that would effectively unite all the colonies, from east to west, had become one of the key issues of federation.

AS FOR THE MILITARY SITUATION, various incidents during the American Civil War, and the continuing threat of American territorial expansion, led a number of people in the Province of Canada and the Maritime colonies to see political union as an effective means of defending their territories against the Americans.

In June 1864, the Macdonald-Cartier administration was defeated by a vote held in the Legislative Council of the Province of Canada. At that time, Macdonald and Brown began discussing how they could avoid holding a general election. Brown agreed to form a new coalition by joining the Conservatives, on the condition that steps be taken toward unifying all the British colonies of North America.

In September 1864, delegates from New Brunswick, Nova Scotia and Prince Edward Island met in Charlottetown, P.E.I., to discuss the possible future union of the Maritime colonies. Representatives from the Province of Canada asked if they could attend and, thanks to careful preparation, managed to convince the Maritime delegates to join with the Province of Canada in an expanded version of federation.

In October of that same year, the men later named "the Fathers of Confederation" (i.e., the delegates attending the Quebec Conference) adopted the Quebec Resolutions, which formed the basis for the future Constitution. One of the provisions included in this draft emphasized a centralized federation, particularly with regard to the economy. There were no public hearings on the Quebec Resolutions, but it was agreed that they should be approved by the legislative bodies of each colony.

In March 1865, the proposed federation was adopted by the Legislative Council of the Province of Canada. In spite of strong opposition, and after a number of delays, it was finally passed in New Brunswick and Nova Scotia. It was rejected by Prince Edward Island and Newfoundland, which could see no economic advantage in it. In December 1866, the drafting of the London Resolutions completed the bill.

In March 1867, the Act of Confederation—officially called the British North America Act—was ratified by the British Parliament, and became effective as of July 1, 1867. The new country was called the Dominion of Canada, comprising New Brunswick, Nova Scotia, and the former Province of Canada, divided into the provinces of Quebec and Ontario.

The British North America Act

The British North America (BNA) Act is the law, passed by the British Parliament, which presided over the founding of the Canadian Confederation. It is the key piece of legislation on which today's Canadian Constitution is built. However, it is also based on older pieces of legislation—such as the Quebec Act of 1774—the constitutional rulings of the Imperial Privy Council and, since 1982, a Charter of Rights and Freedoms and an amending formula. A series of unwritten rules complete the Constitution and put it into practice.

Confederation, as well as being a political compromise, was in some respects also a legal contract between the founding provinces. It was an agreement between four equal partners to create a new level of government that would assume certain powers and be responsible for providing certain services to the general population. Canadian federalism therefore comprised two levels of government—federal and provincial—between which legislative power was divided. However, the text drawn up in 1867 did not specifically define this division of power. There were parts of it that allowed for mutually exclusive interpretations, in favour of federal power or in favour of provincial power.

Confederation:
A Pact between Equals?

From the beginning, French Canadians and English Canadians saw Confederation in a different light. For francophone politicians, intellectuals and historians living in Quebec, it united two nations, two founding peoples. This interpretation of Canada as a pact between equals came from such French-Canadian historians as Lionel Groulx. However, the writings of historians such as Donald Creighton made it clear that, for English Canadians, Confederation was a means of destroying that equality and ensuring that French Canadians would be a minority in political institutions. This original misunderstanding regarding the goals of Confederation is once again evident in today's constitutional discussions.

CHAPTER II

The Initial Struggle for Provincial Autonomy 1867 – 1900

The first signs of conflict between the federal and provincial governments appeared the day after Confederation. From the outset, Ontario was diligent in defending the interests of the provinces, while Quebec remained aloof, not actively participating in the constitutional debate.

In 1867, John A. Macdonald was elected Prime Minister of Canada. Head of the Conservative Party, he was a well-known partisan of a strong, central federal government. Under his leadership, the government intervened regularly in provincial affairs by means of the disallowance clause, which allowed him to quash any provincial law that he deemed contrary to the national interest. Between 1867 and 1896, the federal government used—and abused—this power on more than 60 occasions, much to the irritation of the provinces.

In 1872, Oliver Mowat was elected Premier of Ontario. He was extremely active in the fight for provincial autonomy, and regularly challenged the federal government in court. At least 10 such lawsuits went to the highest court of the time, the Imperial Privy Council. In each instance, the Privy

Council decided in favour of the provinces, thus seriously curtailing the federal government's centralist tendencies. Until the end of the 19th century, the accumulated weight of these decisions was of significant help to the provinces.

During the first 20 years of Confederation, the fight for provincial autonomy was waged by English Canada. Quebec rarely ventured onto the constitutional field, because the provincial Conservative government was politically and economically dependent on Macdonald's federal Conservatives.

After the events involving Louis Riel, a wave of nationalist feeling rose up in Quebec and was used to great advantage by the provincial Liberals; their party leader, Honoré Mercier, was elected Premier in the fall of 1886. Contrary to his Conservative predecessors, Premier Mercier became an ardent defender of provincial autonomy. During his term in office, his brand of autonomy took on many of the characteristics of French-Canadian nationalism.

The Louis Riel Incident

Since the 18th century, the Canadian prairies had been home to both white fur traders and North American Indians. This cohabitation gave rise to a new people—the Métis.

In 1869 and 1870, and then again in 1884 and 1885, the Métis, led by Louis Riel, staged a number of uprisings to protest against the federal government's policy of settling the Canadian West. The rebels were for the most part francophone Catholics, and their resistance became a focal point for the tensions developing between English and French Canadians. Captured by federal forces in 1885, Louis Riel was found guilty by an English-Canadian court and hanged. French Canadians were outraged.

> The Conservatives were called "scoundrels" and the death of Louis Riel became a symbol of French-Canadian oppression by the English-Canadian majority.
>
> Following Louis Riel's death, religious intolerance spread across the country. In 1889 and 1890, the Ontario members of the Equal Rights Association led a vigorous campaign against what they perceived as an inordinate amount of influence wielded by Catholics in Canadian government affairs. Such was the prevailing atmosphere in 1890, when the Manitoba government abolished the use of French in all government institutions and restricted the teaching of Catholicism and French in its schools.

Honoré Mercier's opinions on provincial autonomy were grounded on two main principles. The first was that the federal government had been brought into being by the provinces and, for that reason, they should not be subject to it. The second was that French Canadians had only one government that really spoke for them, and that was the provincial one. This was a relatively new idea for the time. During Honoré Mercier's term in office, these principles gained increasing acceptance; French Canadians no longer believed that the federal government was the "big" government, nor that it was the sole defender of French-Canadian minorities across the country.

In July 1887, in Quebec City, Honoré Mercier called the premiers of the other provinces together in the first federal-provincial meeting since Confederation. Five premiers—all of them Liberals—took part in the meeting. The federal government declined to attend. Even though there was no follow-up to the proposals made at that meeting, the provinces nevertheless showed the federal government that they could unite against it and thus were a force to be reckoned with.

In 1896, Wilfrid Laurier became Prime Minister of Canada. He was more conciliatory, more open to the idea of provincial autonomy than John A. Macdonald had been. A new federal-provincial balance of power was thus established. It simultaneously restricted the federal government's tendencies toward centralization and gave the provinces greater scope to establish their autonomy.

CHAPTER III

The Golden Age of Provincial Autonomy 1900 – 1930

During the first few decades of the 20th century, there was little action on the constitutional front. The federal government rarely intervened in provincial affairs, except during the First World War. In retrospect, this period can be seen as a "golden age" of provincial autonomy.

In 1905, Lomer Gouin was elected Premier of Quebec and continued the work Honoré Mercier had begun, particularly with regard to provincial autonomy. Supported by the other premiers, he requested an increase in federal grants to the provinces. The amount of these grants had not changed since 1867, and they were in no way sufficient for the steadily increasing needs of the provinces.

In 1907, after repeated requests from the provinces, Prime Minister Laurier substantially boosted federal grants. At the same time, he agreed in principle to adjust them in accordance with each province's population, as determined by a regular census. Politically speaking, this shift represented a major victory for the provinces. However, financially speaking, it was simply not enough: although the actual dollar amount went up, the relative percentage of federal grants in provincial budgets progressively decreased, due to the constant increase in provincial expenditures.

In 1912, the federal government introduced a new method of financing, called "conditional grants." Under this new method, the government set aside large sums of money for the provinces; however, these could only be used for specific needs, previously determined by the federal government. This system, which met with no opposition from the provinces at the time, became more firmly entrenched after the Second World War.

The First World War corresponded to the initial stages of centralization, which greatly benefited the federal government. In 1916, it introduced corporate taxes and in 1917, to finance the war effort, a "temporary" tax on private income. The federal government thus became involved in the whole spectrum of taxation, including direct taxes, which until then had been the exclusive right of the provinces. By the time the war was over, the federal government's heavy debt load prevented it from abolishing these two "temporary" taxes, as it had promised. This situation angered the provinces, and taxes became the main bone of contention between the federal and provincial governments.

The Conscription Crisis

In 1917, when voluntary enrollment in the army failed to provide sufficient manpower for the war effort, the federal government introduced conscription. The French Canadians strongly opposed this measure; they objected to the idea of fighting for Great Britain, in an almost exclusively English-speaking army. Their opposition to conscription split the country along linguistic lines. The ensuing crisis was, without doubt, the worst internal conflict the country had ever experienced.

In 1920, Alexandre Taschereau became Premier of Quebec. Starting in 1921, he renewed the fight for a more equitable division of taxes between the federal and provincial governments. He stridently denounced even minor encroachments on areas of provincial jurisdiction, such as highway maintenance, natural resources (a constant source of revenue for the provinces), education and agriculture. He opposed the proposed construction of the St. Lawrence Seaway and, in 1927, he refused to participate in the federal old-age pension program. Like Ontario, Quebec had become a vocal proponent of provincial autonomy.

CHAPTER IV

The Shift toward Centralization 1930 – 1960

The combined effect of the Depression of 1929 and the Second World War disrupted the delicate balance that had existed between the federal and provincial governments since the end of the 19th century, and led to a greater concentration of powers in the hands of the federal government.

In the early 1930s, Canada was going through its most severe economic crisis ever. Unable to remain indifferent in the face of widespread unemployment and deteriorating living conditions, governments were forced to take a more active role in the lives of Canadians. However, the task of providing relief proved immense, and provincial and municipal governments had to ask the federal government for help in setting up new social security and public works programs.

That was the backdrop against which the federal elections of 1935 were held, and against which Richard B. Bennett's Conservative government presented its New Deal: a social and economic reform program largely based on American President Roosevelt's program of the same name. Set up without the consent of the provinces, the new Conservative policy included several laws that encroached on areas of provincial jurisdiction.

In the years that followed, Ontario and Quebec challenged these laws in the federal courts and, one by one, they were quashed.

In the summer of 1935, the leader of the Liberal Party, William Lyon Mackenzie King, was elected Prime Minister of Canada. In response to the ongoing economic crisis, his government suggested setting up an unemployment insurance program. After heated debate, the provinces agreed to let the Constitution be modified so that Mackenzie King could legally establish his new unemployment insurance program, which was introduced in 1941. It was a cornerstone of the federal welfare state, and constituted a significant step toward a centralized federal government.

The Concept of the Welfare State

The fundamental objectives of the welfare state are to "protect" all citizens from the misfortunes of life, such as sickness, old age, unemployment, etc., and to ensure a basic standard of living. The minimum income thus provided is crucial to economic growth during hard times.

From 1939 to 1945, the Second World War gave the federal government even greater scope for intervening in everyday life. The War Measures Act extended its powers and allowed it to collect higher taxes, just as it had done during the First World War. The additional power wielded by the federal government during that period made it aspire to enter several more areas of provincial jurisdiction.

After the war, the federal government—whose finances were in excellent shape, thanks to the post-war boom—went on the offensive: it convened numerous federal-provincial conferences in an attempt to convince the provinces to cede power in areas that had hitherto belonged to them: taxes, education and social programs. These were areas in which federal reforms, such as Unemployment Insurance (1941), Family Allowance (1945) and the Canadian Mortgage and Housing Corporation (1946), had already earned it the support of most Canadians, including those living in Quebec.

In English Canada most provinces, particularly the poorer ones, agreed fairly readily to delegate certain powers to the federal government. In Quebec, the idea met with strong opposition from Maurice Duplessis' conservative government.

Maurice Duplessis and the Union Nationale

In 1942, the nation was once again in the midst of a Conscription Crisis. Although less violent than the first, it created a strong feeling of resentment among French Canadians that, in 1944, led them to elect Maurice Duplessis, leader of the Union Nationale. He would remain Premier of Quebec for the next 15 years. Maurice Duplessis and his government were conservative in their view of Quebec society, advocating traditional, rural, Catholic values. He was bitterly opposed to change, as represented by the trade unions, and resisted encroachment by the federal government. During the 1960s, his term as Premier was referred to as "la grande noirceur" (the blackout) even though, in general, Quebec had been developing at the same rate as other provinces during those years.

In 1947, all provinces except Quebec and Ontario gave the federal government the right to raise tax revenues. Ontario finally gave in to federal pressure five years later, but Quebec categorically refused to comply, in spite of negative financial repercussions.

In 1951, after obtaining the consent of all the provinces, the federal government modified the Constitution to ensure that it had a monopoly on old-age pensions.

In 1953, the government of Quebec and the federal government managed to reach an agreement on the thorny issue of taxes: Quebec was to receive 10% of federal income tax. Politically speaking, this was a small but important victory. It was the first time, since the end of the Second World War, that the federal government had given in to a province's demands.

This period of increasing centralization—from 1930 to 1960—gave rise to two distinct perceptions of Canadian federalism. In English Canada, the more traditional regionalism had gradually given way to a kind of pan-Canadian nationalism. This nationalism was based on the search for a common Canadian identity, within a nation that adhered to the federal model of a welfare state. Quebec took the opposite view. Influenced by the Maurice Duplessis government, it continued to look back to the golden days of provincial autonomy, when central government intervention and social policies were at a minimum. Because of this, Quebec became more isolated than ever from the rest of Canada.

CHAPTER V

Two Kinds of Nationalism Clash 1960 – 1971

It was clear that English and French Canadians did not have a common vision for their country, and they found it hard to reconcile their differing perceptions of Canada. Conflict was inevitable, and the 1960s marked the beginning of a long series of confrontations.

In the early 1960s, the federal government increased its efforts to concentrate power in its own hands. In this, it had been supported by English Canada since the end of the Second World War. Around that time, Quebec's relationship with the federal government underwent a significant change. Abandoning the issue of provincial autonomy, it began to agitate for a new division of power and special status within the Canadian federation.

The constitutional situation was becoming increasingly complex and, at the same time, it began to play a more important role in Canadian politics.

1960 – 1964

In July 1960, barely one month after he was elected, Quebec Premier Jean Lesage presented his government's position on the Constitution. He stated that the federal government should respect the provinces' rights in all their areas of jurisdiction. His government reintroduced the concept of provincial autonomy, turning it into a positive, more action-oriented approach. This basic message would be echoed by all successive Quebec provincial governments.

In 1962, after being re-elected under the slogan "Maîtres chez nous" (masters in our own house), Jean Lesage and his Liberals launched a series of sweeping social reforms that became known as the "Quiet Revolution." This included the creation of a provincial Ministry of Education and the nationalization of the hydroelectric industry. They also began to channel available funds into such organizations as the Société générale de financement (the General Investment Corporation of Quebec) and the Caisse de dépôts et placements (Quebec's deposit and investment fund) for the purpose of provincial development. All these measures served to strengthen Quebec's incipient statehood; at the same time, Quebec abandoned traditional French-Canadian nationalism and opted, instead, for a more active, positive sense of national identity.

In 1964, after lengthy and difficult negotiations, Ottawa granted Quebec an "opting-out" formula, by which any province could refuse to take part in a federal-provincial shared-cost program. Instead, they could set up their own program, and still receive funding from the federal government. Opting out was a right granted to all the provinces, but Quebec was the only one to use this option, withdrawing immediately from approximately 30 federal shared-cost programs. That same year, thanks to this legal mechanism, Quebec set up the Quebec pension plan, the provincial equivalent of the Canada Pension Plan. This major victory for the cause of provincial autonomy gave Quebec special status within Confederation.

It was no longer constrained by the division of powers determined in 1867; rather, it was in a position to demand even greater powers, as it pursued its goal of creating a genuine Québécois state.

1964 – 1968

The highlights of federal-provincial relations in 1965 were the federal government's efforts to repatriate the Constitution (i.e., bring it from London back to Ottawa), and the Fulton-Favreau formula, a legal mechanism by which the Constitution could be amended. In Quebec government circles there were more and more converts to the idea of special status for the province, which would be entrenched in the new Constitution. A number of nationalist provincial ministers—among them René Lévesque—lost no time in publicly expressing their doubts concerning the Fulton-Favreau amending formula.

In the fall of 1965, Premier Lesage travelled through Western Canada, and saw first-hand English Canada's incomprehension with regard to Quebec's burgeoning aspirations. At the same time, expert analysis seemed to indicate that the federal government's proposals did not, in fact, guarantee a new division of power in Quebec's favour once the Constitution had been repatriated. In light of this, Premier Lesage decided to withdraw his support for the amending formula indefinitely and attack on another front: he demanded that, before there was any further discussion of repatriation or an amending formula, a consensus be reached on the issues of power-sharing and recognition of Quebec's special status.

There were some Quebec federalists who felt that, in rejecting the Fulton-Favreau amending formula, Lesage and his government had gone too far. In late 1965, amid considerable public attention, three influential Quebec public figures joined Lester B. Pearson's governing federal Liberals: Pierre Elliott Trudeau, Jean Marchand and Gérard Pelletier.

In the 1966 provincial elections, Daniel Johnson led the Union Nationale to victory with the campaign slogan "Égalité ou indépendance" (Equality or independence). The new premier was more radical and had more nationalist fervour than his predecessor, Jean Lesage. Premier Johnson not only called for an initial consensus on power-sharing, he also wanted the concept of Canada's two founding peoples to be entrenched in the new Constitution.

In August 1967, during his official visit to Montreal's Expo 67, French President Charles de Gaulle spoke from the balcony of City Hall and uttered his famous cry: "Vive le Québec libre" (Long live free Quebec). This incident had an enormous impact on the Quebec independence movement, but it also placed Johnson's government in a difficult situation vis-à-vis an increasingly exasperated English Canada.

In early 1968, Prime Minister Lester B. Pearson appointed Pierre Elliott Trudeau to work on the constitutional portfolio. Finding the federal government too conciliatory in dealing with a province that had become a threat to national unity, Trudeau issued Quebec a three-point agenda. First, at Trudeau's request, the federal government planned to amend the Constitution so as to include a charter of rights and freedoms aimed at protecting Canadian linguistic minorities. Second, he suggested a number of ways to streamline federal institutions, including plans to reform the Supreme Court and Senate. Power-sharing was not discussed until the third point. However, it seemed that special status for Quebec within Confederation, or any mention of the "two founding peoples" concept, was now out of the question.

1968 – 1971

In June 1968, Pierre Elliott Trudeau was elected Prime Minister of Canada. Before that time René Lévesque, a fervent Quebec nationalist, had left Lesage's Liberal Party; shortly thereafter, he formed a new movement called the Parti Québécois. His intention was to rally those people who believed that there was no place for an independent-minded Quebec within the Canadian federation.

Trudeau's government wanted to resolve the Quebec "problem" once and for all. Trudeau was convinced that Canada-wide linguistic concessions would satisfy Quebec's constitutional demands. In 1969, his government passed the Official Languages Act, which made English and French the two official languages in Canada. Although designed first and foremost to promote bilingualism in Canada, this Act also required that federal services throughout the country be provided in French. The response from English Canada was not overwhelmingly enthusiastic.

The Quebec Liberal Party, and its young leader, Robert Bourassa, won a landslide victory in the 1970 provincial elections. Premier Bourassa's government was avowedly federalist and was sure it could reach an agreement with Trudeau's governing Liberals.

In the fall of 1970, hamstrung by the kidnappings undertaken by the Front de libération du Québec (FLQ), Robert Bourassa and his cabinet finally handed matters over to the federal government. In order to restore peace in the province, it invoked the War Measures Act, and more than 500 suspected FLQ supporters were arrested. Although the October Crisis did not directly affect the constitutional debate, many separatists saw it as an unacceptable use of power by the federal government.

Constitutional negotiations began again in early 1971. An agreement in principle between the provinces and the federal government gave rise to the Victoria Charter. It included a charter of rights and freedoms as well as plans to reform federal institutions such as the Supreme Court and the Senate. Also, for the first time ever, the new Charter granted Quebec an official veto on Constitutional amendments.

In February 1971, a meeting was held to finalize the details of the Victoria Charter. One of the issues under discussion was power-sharing in the area of social policy. Over the next few months, there was growing opposition to the Charter in Quebec. Many experts and analysts saw it as an unacceptable setback to Quebec's aspirations, since they believed it did not grant Quebec sufficient autonomy in the implementation of social policy.

In June 1971, at a conference held in Victoria, B.C., Robert Bourassa's government bowed to public opinion in Quebec and rejected outright all the federal government's proposals contained in the Charter. At that point, the various governments decided to put constitutional negotiations aside for at least several years.

CHAPTER VI

The Constitutional Merry-Go-Round 1971 – 1990

After the Victoria Charter was rejected, constitutional negotiations were put on hold. Both Quebec and the federal government had other issues to deal with: the former was preoccupied with language-related issues and the latter was wrestling with economic problems, such as inflation and the energy crisis.

Indeed, it wasn't until there was an upsurge of separatist feelings in the Western provinces, and a sovereigntist government was elected in Quebec in 1976, that the federal government reopened constitutional negotiations.

1971 – 1982

In 1973 – 74, the first energy crisis hit Canada. In the Western provinces— and particularly in Alberta, which has large oil deposits—there was a revival of regionalist sentiment, marked by demands for provincial autonomy. In an effort to deal with the crisis, the federal government set a ceiling on oil prices in order to keep them uniformly low across the country. Alberta, which had hoped to profit from the rise in world oil prices, opposed this new federal policy. The Prairie provinces experienced a political awakening once they realized the profits that could be made from exploiting their natural resources. Separatist feeling remained an important factor in relations between the Western provinces and the federal government right up until the 1980s.

In 1976, Pierre Elliott Trudeau's Liberal government was even more determined to repatriate the Constitution, this time emphasizing that it could act unilaterally without the consent of the provinces.

Robert Bourassa's provincial Liberals had not responded forcefully enough to the turmoil surrounding the passage of the notorious Bill 22, and consequently their popularity plummeted. Bourassa called an early election, and asked the Quebec electorate for a clear mandate to oppose the federal government's plans to unilaterally repatriate the Constitution.

Bill 22 and the Language Policy for Schools

As the 1960s drew to a close, language issues were a hot topic in Quebec. Demonstrations calling for the primacy of the French language were organized across the province. For example, many people felt that immigrants should be required to register their children in French schools. In 1974, Bourassa's government decided to settle the question once and for all by introducing the notorious Bill 22. Once law, French became the only official language in Quebec, and access to English schools for the children of immigrants was restricted by means of English assessment tests. The situation became tense. Anglophones (i.e., people whose mother tongue is English) and allophones (i.e., people whose mother tongue is neither English nor French) felt they had been humiliated and their rights infringed upon. Francophones (i.e., people whose mother tongue is French) felt that the government had not done enough to protect the French language. The widespread dislike of this new law was part of the reason why Bourassa and his Liberals were defeated in the 1976 elections.

In November 1976, René Lévesque and the Parti Québécois beat Robert Bourassa's Liberals in the provincial elections. René Lévesque's separatist government went back to the roots of Quebec's struggle against centralization by stating that the federal government should respect the autonomy of the provinces in all areas under their jurisdiction.

In 1977, the federal government and the provinces opened yet another round of constitutional negotiations. Several meetings were held, but no agreement was reached.

In 1979, there was yet another dramatic rise in oil prices; the economic situation deteriorated and tensions mounted between the federal government and the Western provinces. At that time, Pierre Trudeau's Liberals lost the May 1979 federal elections, and Joe Clark, leader of the Conservative Party, became the new Prime Minister of Canada—although not for long. Taking advantage of the constitutional impasse, the Quebec government set forth its proposal for sovereignty-association, calling for an equal partnership with the rest of Canada. It planned to hold a referendum to gauge popular support for the proposal.

In February 1980, less than one year after they had been defeated, Trudeau's Liberals were back in power—mostly on the strength of the Quebec vote, since the federal Liberals didn't win a single seat west of Manitoba.

Both Trudeau's government in Ottawa and René Lévesque's Parti Québécois government in Quebec marshalled their forces for the referendum on sovereignty-association that was set for May 1980. Throughout the referendum campaign, Prime Minister Trudeau held out the promise of a "renewed federalism" if the No-side won, although he didn't offer any specific details.

On May 20, 1980, the No-side won 60% of the vote. Flushed with victory, the federal government decided to accelerate the repatriation of the Constitution.

By October 1980, Trudeau's government had still not reached an agreement with the provinces, and so it decided to act alone, and repatriate the Constitution without their consent. In April 1981, eight provinces, including Quebec, joined together to thwart its plans. They asked the Supreme Court of Canada to determine if unilateral repatriation of the Constitution was in fact legal.

The Supreme Court of Canada handed down its decision in September 1981. It declared that although unilateral repatriation of the Constitution was legal, it ran counter to Canadian constitutional convention, according to which the federal government and the provinces must reach an agreement before modifying the Constitution.

In November 1981, at the end of yet another round of negotiations, the nine provinces in English Canada managed, at the last minute, to reach an agreement with the federal government. They agreed to repatriate the Canadian Constitution and to modify it to include, among other documents, the Charter of Rights and Freedoms so dear to Prime Minister Trudeau. Only one province did not enter into the agreement: Quebec.

In Ottawa, on April 17, 1982, Queen Elizabeth II officially proclaimed the 1982 Constitution Act, which was based on the agreement reached a few months earlier between the federal government and nine provinces. Quebec was the only province that did not sign the Constitution; that day, it flew its flags at half-mast.

1982 – 1990

At this time, a number of new arrivals on the political scene led to yet another round of constitutional negotiations.

In September 1984, the Conservatives came to power in Ottawa, and Brian Mulroney became Prime Minister of Canada. In December of the following year, Robert Bourassa was elected Premier of Quebec, and brought the Liberals back to power.

Prime Minister Mulroney favoured a conciliatory approach to federal-provincial relations. One of his main political goals was to bring Quebec back to the bargaining table so that it would sign the new Canadian Constitution. Premier Bourassa wanted nothing better; in 1986, he set forth five conditions required before his government would sign.

In June 1987, a first ministers' conference was held at Meech Lake, north of Ottawa, to discuss these five conditions. Quebec seemed much less demanding than it had been under Jean Lesage or Daniel Johnson, and so all five conditions were unanimously accepted.

In fact, of the five conditions laid down by the Quebec government, only one dealt with the division of powers, and that was in the area of immigration, where an administrative agreement already existed between Quebec and the federal government. However, the Accord had to be approved by the House of Commons and all provincial legislatures within three years, or it would not be valid.

Thanks to the Meech Lake Accord, Premier Bourassa accepted the 1982 Constitution Act *in toto*, without demanding any major changes. At this point, his entire constitutional strategy was summed up by a clause in the new Meech Lake Accord that mentioned the term "distinct society." He believed that, in future negotiations, this clause would finally allow him to obtain the division of powers for which Quebec had been waiting for 30 years. However, time passed, the weight of expert opinion grew, and people came to realize that the concept of a distinct society had no real bearing on the division of powers.

The Meech Lake Accord: A "Distinct Society" Clause and Other Demands Made by Quebec

One of the most controversial items in the Meech Lake Accord was the clause stating that the 1982 Constitution Act would be interpreted in light of "the recognition that Quebec constitutes within Canada a distinct society." It also stated that governments at the federal and provincial levels should preserve the bilingual nature of Canada. Furthermore, the agreement established the opting-out formula, gave the provinces the right to review nominees to the Supreme Court and Senate, and granted increased powers to the provinces—particularly to Quebec—in the area of immigration. For many English Canadians, the concept of a distinct society ran counter to their notion of a country founded on equal rights for all, as laid out in the Charter of Rights and Freedoms. Why should the people of Quebec have the right to form a distinct society, or have special status, and not the native peoples?

Between 1987 and 1990, yet another language-related storm raged in Quebec, this time centred around Bill 101. This bill, passed when René Lévesque was in power, stipulated that French predominate in all areas of public life. However, since the Liberals had come to power in 1985, the English-speaking population in Quebec had regularly expressed their opposition to the bill, which they felt was too restrictive.

In December 1988, the Supreme Court of Canada handed down a decision in this regard. Based on the new Constitution of 1982, which Quebec had still not signed, it declared certain provisions of Bill 101— such as those dealing with public signs—to be illegal. Francophones in Quebec organized a huge demonstration in support of Bill 101. The message to Robert Bourassa and his government was clear: this law should remain basically unchanged!

In response to the Supreme Court's ruling, Premier Bourassa invoked the "notwithstanding clause" contained in the 1982 Constitution Act. This clause allows a province, in certain cases, to opt out of the new Constitution. In English Canada, there was growing exasperation with the notion of a distinct society, and a few anti-French demonstrations took place outside Quebec.

By June 1990, Manitoba and Newfoundland had still not ratified the Meech Lake Accord. Since the legal deadline had passed, it became, *de facto*, null and void. In the end, Bourassa's constitutional strategy had ended in defeat for Quebec.

CHAPTER VII

The Constitutional Debate Since 1990

The Meech Lake fiasco severely weakened Robert Bourassa's government. In Quebec, popular discontent flared into ardent nationalism. Although the failure of the Meech Lake Accord was primarily a reflection of English Canada's exasperation with Quebec's demands, the native peoples—who had been taking a more active part in negotiations with the federal and provincial governments since the end of the 1970s—saw it as a chance to advance their own cause.

In May 1990, Lucien Bouchard resigned from Brian Mulroney's cabinet. Indeed, he left the Conservative Party altogether and, in conjunction with other former Conservative MPs from Quebec, he founded the Bloc Québécois, a separatist party dedicated to defending the interests of Quebec in Ottawa.

In June 1990, immediately after the failure of Meech Lake, Bourassa's government announced that it would not participate in any constitutional negotiations until further notice. Quebec's National Assembly (the equivalent of a provincial legislature in other provinces) set up a commission of inquiry to look into Quebec's constitutional options. The

Bélanger-Campeau Commission convened in the fall of 1990. During the hearings, the idea of political sovereignty—which had been dropped after the No-side won in the 1980 referendum—was raised once again.

In January 1991, Quebec's Liberal Party published the Allaire Report, stating its new, post-Meech Lake position on constitutional matters. The report stated that Canadian federalism in its current form could not satisfy the aspirations of the people of Quebec. It advocated expanding Quebec's areas of jurisdiction through greater decentralization of federal power, and recommended that a new constitutional agreement be reached with the rest of Canada.

In its report tabled in March 1991, the Bélanger-Campeau Commission concluded that Quebec had only two remaining options: decentralized federalism, along with increased powers for Quebec, or else straightforward political sovereignty. The Commission stated that a referendum on Quebec's constitutional future should be held no later than the fall of 1992.

On June 20, 1991, Quebec's National Assembly enacted legislation defining the process by which Quebec's political and constitutional future would be determined and calling for a referendum on sovereignty before October 26, 1992.

During the summer of 1991, the Spicer Commission, also known as the "Citizen's Forum on the Constitution," tabled its report. Commissioned by the federal government, this massive public opinion survey consulted mostly English Canadians, and was further proof of the incompatible political views held by Quebec and the rest of the country.

Shortly after these reports were tabled, Mulroney's Conservative government decided that it would draw up a new Constitution before the fall of 1992. For one year, from 1991 to 1992, it held more public consultations in an attempt to find some common ground between Quebec, English Canada and the native peoples.

The Arrival of the Native Peoples on the Political Scene

Starting in the 1960s, the native peoples realized that they could improve their situation through political organization, and groups dedicated to defending native interests sprang up across the country. In the 1970s, they focused on government acknowledgment of their many land claims, covering large areas of Canada. The 1982 Constitution Act recognizes the existence of these rights, but states that they must be negotiated separately with each native group. During the 1980s, feeling dissatisfied with the attention paid to Quebec's claims to provincial autonomy, the native peoples began to demand a certain amount of political autonomy of their own. At the beginning of the 1990s, they took advantage of the Meech Lake fiasco to take a seat at the constitutional negotiating table. With English Canada's blessing, they used their position to claim certain territorial rights as well as greater autonomy in native affairs.

During the summer of 1992, Premier Bourassa privately withdrew his support for the recommendations contained in the Allaire Report—even though they had been endorsed by his own party in 1991. Instead, he waited for the federal government's next constitutional offering. In early August, convinced that Quebec and the rest of Canada could reach a consensus, he agreed to return to the bargaining table.

On August 28, 1992, at a conference in Charlottetown, P.E.I., the federal government, the provincial governments and the native leaders agreed on plans to overhaul the Canadian Constitution. Contrary to the Meech Lake Accord, the Charlottetown Accord included reforms that affected not only the people of Quebec (the "distinct society" clause) but the entire population of Canada (reforms to the Senate and the Supreme Court) including the native peoples (increased rights for self-government).

The Charlottetown Accord did not really offer anything new to Quebec. The distinct society clause was circumscribed by a number of related provisions and, although there was a general intent to decentralize, each transfer of power had to be negotiated and agreed upon, preventing Quebec from achieving an equal share of power.

On October 26, 1992, the Charlottetown Accord was the subject of a pan-Canadian referendum, and it was rejected both inside and outside Quebec. Immediately thereafter, nationalist sentiment, which had been running high in Quebec since the defeat of the Meech Lake Accord, fell like a stone.

In October 1993, Jean Chrétien led the Liberals to victory in the federal elections thanks to massive electoral support in Ontario and the Atlantic provinces. Lucien Bouchard and the Bloc Québécois took the majority of seats in Quebec, while Preston Manning and the Reform Party did the same in the Western provinces. This conservative and reactionary right-wing party was born out of traditional Western discontent with the Ontario/Quebec monopolization of federal policies. The Reform Party opposed government intervention in most areas, and advocated dismantling the federal welfare state. The Conservatives had become extremely unpopular due to numerous economic and political blunders, and so managed to win only two seats in the whole country.

In the fall of 1994, Jacques Parizeau and the Parti Québécois won a slim majority in the provincial elections. The new premier promised the electorate that he would hold a referendum on sovereignty before the end of 1995.

In December 1994, Parizeau's government tabled draft legislation on sovereignty, "to resolve once and for all the constitutional problem with which Quebec has been wrestling for many generations."

Starting in February 1995, the people of Quebec were invited to take part in public forums to discuss the possible foundation of a new country. The problems raised in these forums went far beyond the mere question of sovereignty.

In March 1995, the National Commission on the Future of Quebec was asked to synthesize the forum data. In its report, made public in April 1995, it emphasized the necessity of combining plans for political sovereignty with an all-encompassing social policy.

On June 12, 1995, Jacques Parizeau (Parti Québécois), Lucien Bouchard (Bloc Québécois) and Mario Dumont (Action Démocratique du Québec) met in Quebec City to sign a three-way agreement. The key element in this agreement was a proposal for a new economic and political partnership between a sovereign Quebec and Canada.

In September 1995, Parizeau's government tabled the referendum question and the bill on the future of Quebec. This bill provided for a declaration of sovereignty, preceded by a formal offer of economic and political partnership with Canada, and the drawing up of a Quebec constitution.

On October 30, 1995, the people of Quebec narrowly rejected sovereignty-association, with 50.6% of the votes going to the No-side, and 49.4% going to the Yes-side.

Printed
in November 1996
by AGMV « L'IMPRIMEUR »
Cap-Saint-Ignace, Quebec
Canada G0R 1H0